Teenage TALES

Also by Jerry Scott and Jim Borgman

Zits: Sketchbook 1
Growth Spurt: Zits Sketchbook 2
Don't Roll Your Eyes at Me, Young Man!: Zits Sketchbook 3
Are We an "Us"?: Zits Sketchbook 4
Zits Unzipped: Zits Sketchbook 5
Busted!: Zits Sketchbook 6
Road Trip: Zits Sketchbook 7

Treasuries
Humongous Zits
Big Honkin' Zits
Zits: Supersized

Teenage TALES

Zits® Sketchbook No. 8

by JERRY SCOTT and JIM BORGMAN™

**Andrews McMeel
Publishing**

Kansas City

Zits® is syndicated internationally by King Features Syndicate, Inc. For information, write King Features Syndicate, Inc., 888 Seventh Avenue, New York, New York 10019.

04 05 06 07 08 BBG 10 9 8 7 6 5 4 3 2 1

ISBN: 0-7407-5426-2

Library of Congress Control Number: 2003113252

Zits® may be viewed online at
www.kingfeatures.com.

━━━ **ATTENTION: SCHOOLS AND BUSINESSES** ━━━

Andrews McMeel books are available at quantity discounts with bulk purchase for educational, business, or sales promotional use. For information, please write to: Special Sales Department, Andrews McMeel Publishing, 4520 Main Street, Kansas City, Missouri 64111.

Per Isabella, con amore.

—J.S

To Katie Carl. Thanks for making it fun.

—J.B.

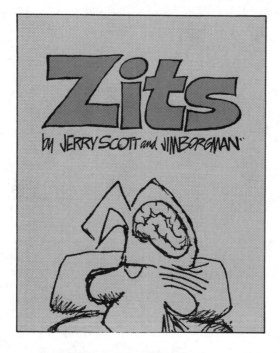

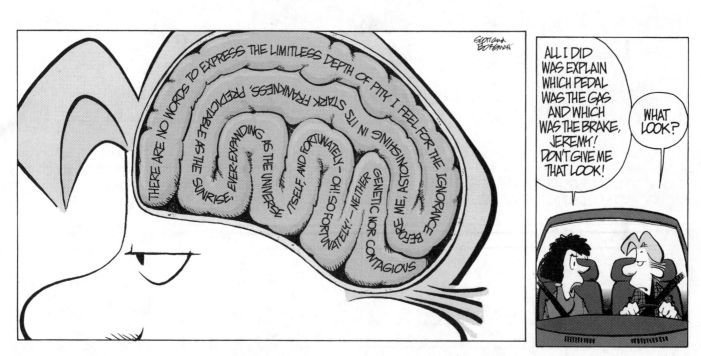

9

11

18

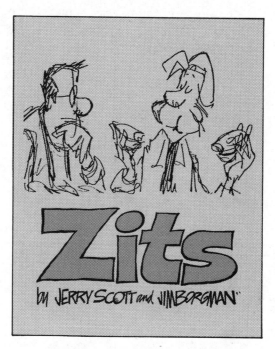

WHAT'S WITH THE NEW LOOK?

I COULDN'T MAKE OUT THE COOKING INSTRUCTIONS ON THIS BOX OF MACARONI, SO I'M WEARING YOUR MOTHER'S READING GLASSES ON TOP OF MY REGULAR GLASSES.

DON'T WORRY... I'LL TAKE THEM OFF ONCE I GET DINNER GOING.

THAT'S A POP TART BOX AND YOU'RE HOLDING IT UPSIDE DOWN.

THIS IS TORTURE

WE SIT IN THIS CLASSROOM FOR 55 MINUTES EVERY DAY, AND NOTHING INTERESTING EVER HAPPENS!

WELL, *ALMOST* NOTHING

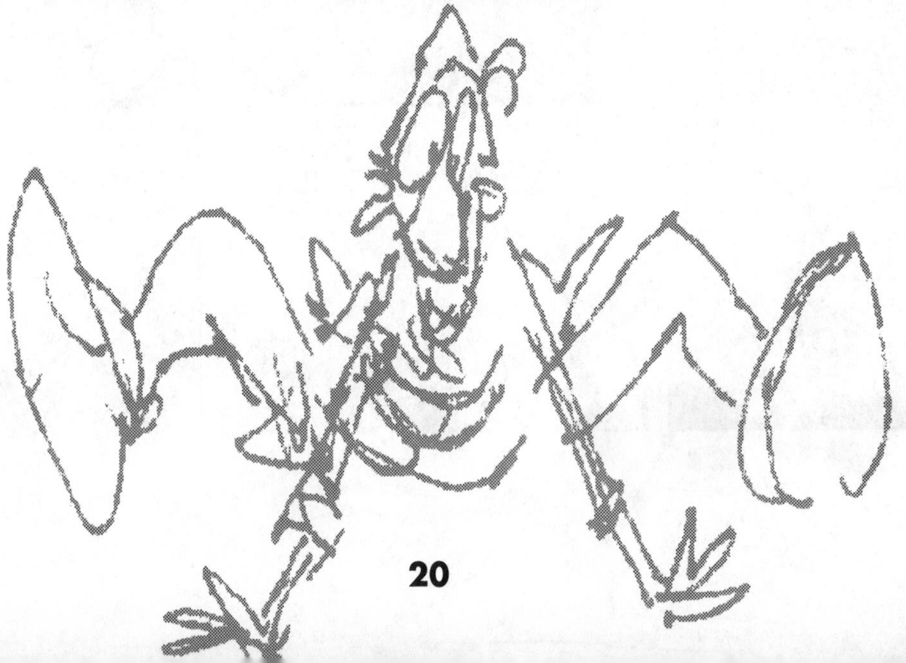

SCOTT AND BORGMAN

21

22

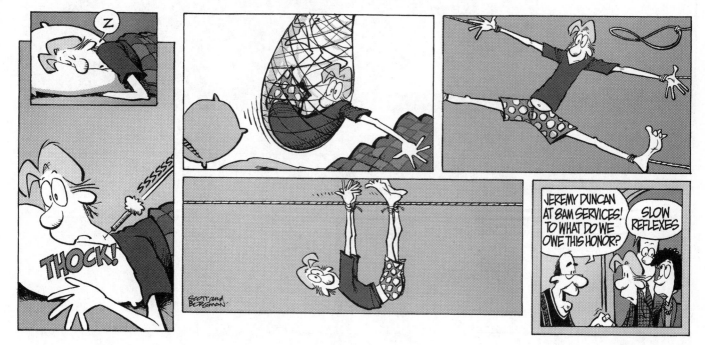

24

28

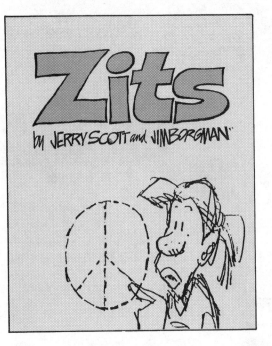

33

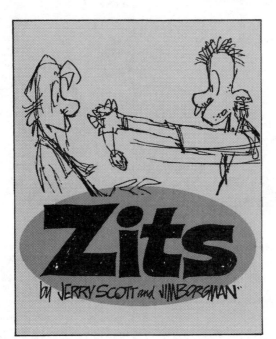

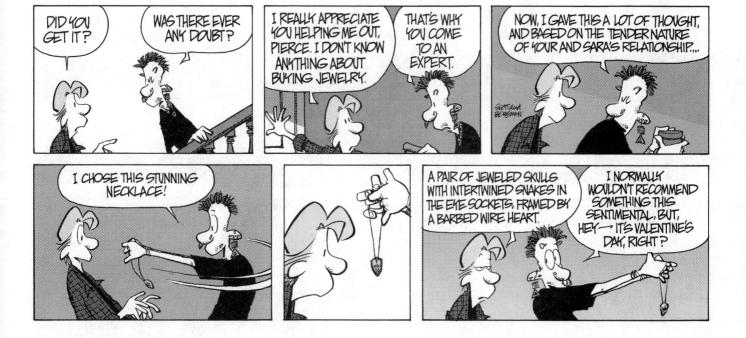

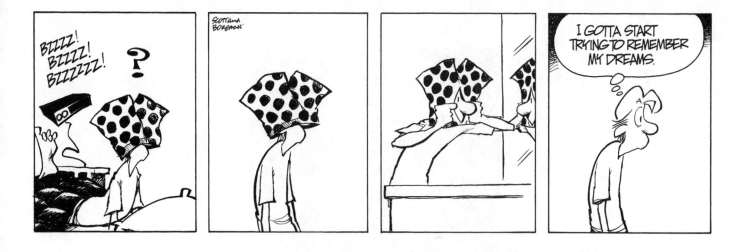

37

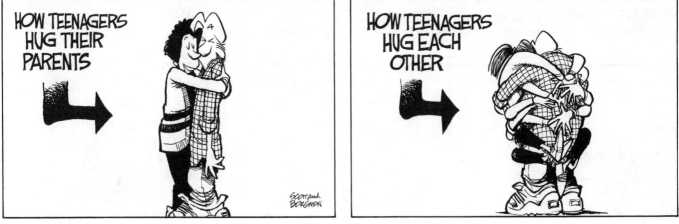

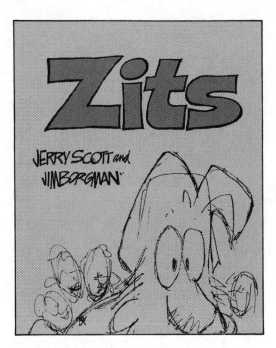

42

45

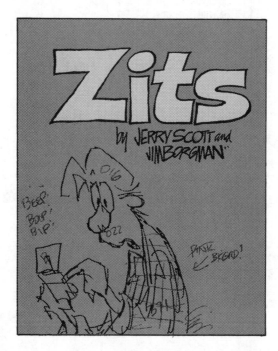

48

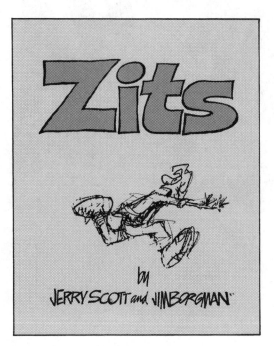

62

63

66

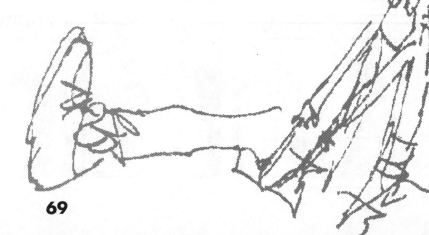

74

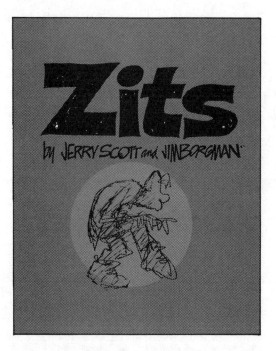

78

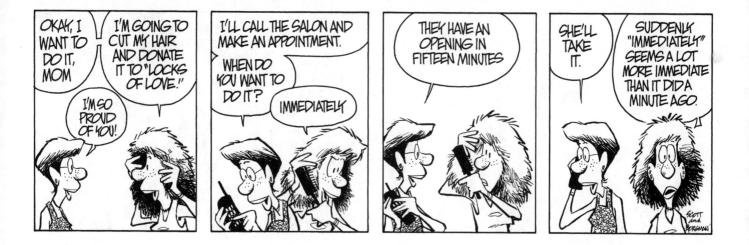

84

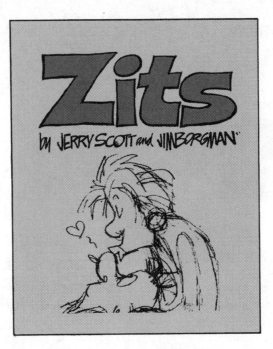

87

90

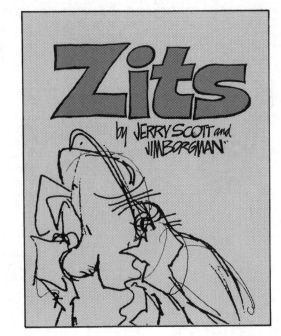

95

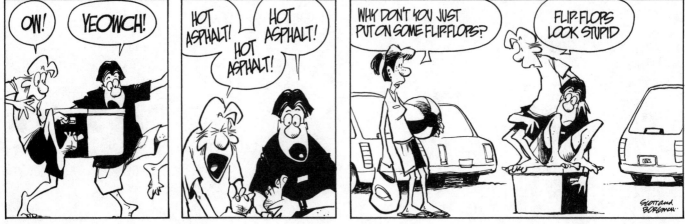

103

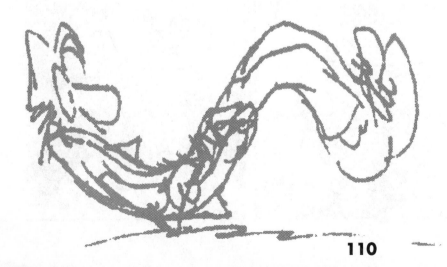

116

119

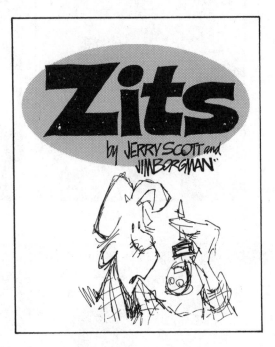

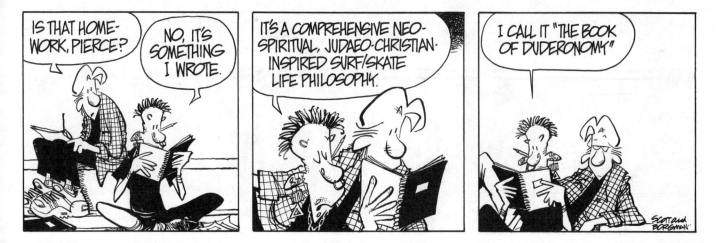

127